SWEET BEAST

SWEET BEAST

poems by Gabriella R. Tallmadge

THP

Tallmadge, Gabriella R.
1ˢᵗ edition

ISBN: 9781949487060
Library of Congress Control Number: 2021931314

Interior design by Matt Mauch
Cover art by Aniko
Cover design by Aniko and Joel Coggins
Editing by Matt Mauch and Sara Lefsyk

Trio House Press, Inc.
Ponte Vedra Beach, FL

To contact the author, send an email to tayveneese@gmail.com.

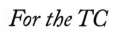

For the TC

Table of Contents

Marriage An Animal Language

When we touch it's animals.
We live in dens, snouts and ends
in the dirt. We frog-eared,
we lick the black off plums.

We sweet? We beast? Ancient,
the memory. Call from an outer face.
We talk in leaf—thought, spine, millions.
I am above you, so below. I grow

of you. Antler, knuckle, snake—cell fall
away from cell, show bone, show meat.
Cape of husk and shell. You are my home,
skin beneath my skin. Cicada hum inside

me nesting near ten years.
In our den we animals we sweet.
We eat limes color of money—
hatch and bloom our blood like seeds.

I

Écorché with Terminal Ballistics

To yawn a wound moon-whole,
first arrange the muscles and the bones.

Understand the skin's stretched canvas,
the instruments behind, their purpose.

Once flayed, all can be revealed:
The relationship between flesh

and the application of a bullet. How
to aid cavitation. The .223 produces

a broad but shallow channel—
avoid the shoulder bones,

stay within gelatinous vitals. A tumbling
55-grain centerfire cartridge will splinter

on impact, separate from its gilded-metal
jacket. For this effect, upset

the round so as to yaw
within the tissue, fragment

at the cannelure. Water hammer
is called hydrolic shock. The wave

of trauma that travels from contact
to distant nerve centers, disrupting

electrical impulses. Cuff-like hemorrhages
blown out in the brain, like

a shorted fuse. Lights out. Collapse,
then coma, then expiration.

Bullets born in twin sets will increase
this likelihood. As do exit wounds.

Dual holes as a means to drain a vessel
is the most basic principle of physics.

But here's a hidden path between scalp
and skull. It will accept a bullet

and guide it over the ridge of bone
without punching through to brain.

And a shot falling low into the heart
will allow blood to be locked

in the locomotive muscles—meaning,
the target will continue to run.

If magnesium is applied,
and a tracer is made, the wound

will glow—shine a light backwards
to illuminate the face of the one who made it.

A bullet sketches a rainbow before it hits.

He tells me this. I can't forget.

The Hypnotist Suggests the Word *Hunger*

Pangs my body knows. Know broken window. Know fifty fists. Know Ferris wheel stretching its legs in my chest. *I can see our house from here.* The white gate swung wide. I can see inside—glasses of milk sweat on every counter. And the glasses glow like votive candles, they hum like columns of rain. Each glass of milk a tarot card, the train behind a bride. *They say the body is a carnival, is one Sunday from Epiphany.* I dream his body is a string of rosary beads, he never speaks, just clinks each notch of spine. How could I turn away from him? How could I face morning with its talk of resurrection, boulders rolled away and then nothing. The well of this burn, how beastly I burned. To unkink the wind, to undress the bones from their trench of marrow. I close my eyes and it's close—that which I would give him, that which I took. A dream in which I scalp the head from comets as a way to say   *I wanted.*

Poem Beginning with a Line from Levis

As if we're put on the earth to forget the ending,
I'm arrested each time I see them—

bodies of dogs and coyotes on the road.

Their static figures against the cruise control,
the sustained speed, indifferent wheels

kneading them over and the lack of recognition.

No flinch or yelp, no one stopping
the car to marvel at deadness,

the set precedence. The dogs anonymous

now as asphalt, highway weeds, the air.
Common bodies lacking actual energy,

but they're shocking—their done aura, a history

instantly interesting. I wonder
if there was such a thing as loneliness

to a coyote. The one with the open mouth,

who had tried to cross the interstate,
smelled the other side, had wild thoughts

pulling her across the painted parallel lines,

had blood or birth or sex willing her forward,
who failed. I wonder if someone will miss

the red spaniel, thought the dog was unique,

an individual with preference and personality,

but how it is equal to its end and no longer

any particular it inhabited. I project

on them my own feeling of being derailed,
taken out from the trajectory of a plan,

surprised with violence which overtook

what was the only ceiling of my life—
the sky. Never casting much shadow,

the dogs intersect two lanes, modest

amongst chaos—rude against the rough
exhaust, commuter cars. I fear they don't mean

what I want them to, but I am small

to the task of my life. How do I mean
oblivion when I can't say the words *it's over?*

Hypnotic at high speed, I forgot

where I was headed. The cars
all face the same direction. I miss when

I didn't know the eroding wave of traffic

pulling overtop soft mouths, smoothing
molars into paint. Wheels churn over

a coyote's form until it isn't one anymore,
is now everything and not lost.

Helmand Province

In your last letter,
you said you're living at Kajaki Dam,
where the Helmand River is a muscular sash.
Mostly, you see sandbags in the windows
and watch the thin shoulders of the road
as you drive down the hill to a post
called *The Shrine*.

Your future is blank
like a pony's wall eye, as holy,
as sick as that pony
as it's led, step by step
past the fence.

I've never named a horse
and had to bury it.
I remember every dog I had
that ran away from home.
These little sores
are everywhere inside me.

I'm so filled up with January,
a mum chamber lodged with sleep.
In dreams, you're killed
and I see your high-walled wilderness
reaching higher than the light does.

Once, before you left for Afghanistan,
I researched the time it takes between death
and family notification. I fantasized for days,
fit my face with grief—it never took.
Because where would I keep that violence?
You expiring like an animal.
Bullets humming to themselves like bees.

Marriage a Pair of Wild Dogs

Hoard & tooth. House & bone.
Hounded. Held. Hound us,
we bite. We, bitten, house

a crown of teeth.
We own no wish, we
need. We are hungry.

Language dead, we bond
to dogs who roam
with us, dig us

from our silent home.
We come from wounding,
born harmful, bow-tight. We

are hours asked *why?*
Every increment of *how*
crowds the gangway

of our throats
but we have no word
for *hurry* just the snow

come hard at dawn.
We are rutted in
our empty, our migrant,

our lost. For this we make
small dangers. None other
breeds to loss.

Parasomnia

What is it that you see when you wake
in the middle of sleep? The veil over
your eyes so the next morning

you don't remember saying *Did they
shoot me?* You don't remember the night
I startled it as you slept and you

almost shot me. Endlessly
on-call in Afghanistan, your hours
were only punctuated with sleep.

Muscle memory learned in Kajaki,
Musa Qala, near Sangin, in Marjah,
at FOB Zeebrugge and Whitehouse,

even at Camp Leatherneck led you to
where your gun was kept. That look in
your eyes said you were still asleep.

I wanted to ask who I was in your dream.
The loud sky? The Pashtun man who eyeballed
you before they rushed your post? Boots

running over themselves? The Jerusalem mule
limping along riderless before it knelt in the road
and exploded? The only thing

my hands could do was touch your chest
and tell you *It's me*. Cold, you came back
down. Fell like a pruned rose back to sleep.

I turned into a birth-wet fawn, flattened
in the steppe grass. I laid still, waited for those
shadows in your head to retract their fangs.

Frida Kahlo, *The Little Deer*, 1946

What has cast on me
                    warped vision,   has throbbed
                    my head

with drones? I am sewn to,   I am soldered—

I beg to be threaded through with arrows.
I want the pain to be obvious.

What wreckage, such freedom—
                    wounds declaring themselves
                    with fletchings. Finally

there could be a fixed distance

between grief and its origin. Containing the ask

of wound, how it eats past and past

                    the vanishing point—projecting itself

                    as infinite extension.

If wound had an architecture,
if it had a grave to feed branches into,

if it could be calculated to be 2.9 miles from horizon—

would it be real then?
                  Would wound be done?

I wed myself
           with want
              of face for it.

To bolt my guts to gravity.

Ground the inanimate, unlimited.

Fracturing Travelogue

*

Another blank wire hanger.
Every year you disappear, leave me
standing in the parking lot, my sendoff
flossed out by the wind, further out
towards the Pacific, cleaving the ocean-
wide sky of *see you.*

*

The moon, its one lengthy crater
getting longer. The moon, a lit gong.
The pressure of space stacked on space
cracks seams in its cold hollow. Hear
the peal solo, the bright split.

*

Our apartment carpet freshly vacuumed,
but only one set of footprints to our bedroom.
They are the pocks of quiet draft,
the baying lack of you.

*

The book-pressed look of birds on trees—
flip the page, a bird knifes through
the white-gray lilt of wind. Behind the window,
the world rages in quiet.

*

Am I on fire or damp? Am I the bright
white boat out too far?

*

I imagine you resting silently with me.
My organs settling into their dark cages,
my brain pacing in front of its shut door.

The Body's Law Transcribed from Darkness

Form we penetrate, endless becoming
    finite, even intimate. Ours, even.
Each body doled out whole, even if

    missing a swatch of flesh in the mouth,
or bone found mid-made at birth.
    Darkness poured over each cluster of us,

culture of what will become a nose, bouquet of hair—
    diligent in where to keep adding flesh.
Sometimes holding back, sometimes

    subtracting. Bless the darkness
inside each woman. The womb—deep doll box—
    and uterus work in darkness on us,

only to be given over to the bright
    tang of light. Each body expected to adjust,
even accept light as what is at our source.

    Darkness caught trundled in with fear and fable:
Claw-of-rat, out of time, locked. Each body
    taught to listen for a whistle in the dark,

to find dawn. But we are muck, in us is fecund.
    The body came from the return of blue, of black,
the body's blood route. Nothing looks red

    on the inside, no color but black, no eyes,
no light, no absence. Each cell many-minded
    in composition with the others also in darkness.

Each bud's willingness a law at our birth.
    Formless, at first. As one fish is a beacon,
sending a low pulse to her others, they become.

And like the fish in the fog of thousands, the body
becomes. Out and emerged, the body,
    light from dark, is glow. We give each nameless

ache our own. We ask ourselves to not
    be afraid of what can't be seen. The future
of our bodies has already been written:

    Wreck, bullet, sleep. Tattoos predating skin.
To each body, darkness gifts this.
    We must tessellate the dark inside

and translate it. The blind corners become
    less sharp when we close our eyes—
call the edges of the deep before us *home*.

What Apocalypse

I thought the world might end there.
The supermarket cart slip rattled like a tin shelf
and the twenty screaming grackles dotted a nearby bush.

Prey animals stay alive through fear.

In this life, a man dies and it means nothing
to a blackbird. We hang meaning on them like a gold crucifix.
Should they consider themselves omens,
idols scalloped from an outer space blackness?
They live in no kingdom but death's.

"*All birds* are sick," my mother once said.

I saw the grackles last night after shutting my eyes.
The light was headed back to the surface of the sun,
ponds of ice relaxed to cold streams.
The birds glowed blue, their eyes gelatinous, after-lit
from watching ice. They pushed off into night like glaciers.

I felt the texture of their wordlessness.

This man, his face finished above me,
his hands a sea enshrouding me. His body on mine
is a wave finishing its form. Each night,

I am pressed deeper into the earth.

Last night, the cold-bitten grasses were unread and still.
They knew all they needed. They were awake
in a kind of eyeless listening, pondering, pausing
only to die. They hooped their blades towards the living earth.

I tunneled further.

The man came back to me. He's come back alive.

The machine of this month is run on the earth's electrical urges.
Thunderheads are violent with light.

Nebraska City

In Nebraska City, Nebraska, where I am setting off
the basement's smoke alarm, he is calling from California,

saying he's lost ground. He calls to say he forgot to feed the dog,
take himself outside. He is afraid of what's featured

in the amphitheater of his mind. I am in a basement
letting the eggs burn. I am looking out a half-moon window

beginning to brim with smoke. I have walked willingly
into the bridge of a downing ship. As if the sky were smoke,

we are. His voice a splintered plank. He is drunk.
I am looking out onto the Corso imagining the Missouri River,

the brittle trees, the taxidermy bison and their desiccated clods
of fur in the Lewis and Clark Museum. I am not removing

the barrowed skillet from the stove. The alarm is shrill
in the basement of this brick house, though the residents

above cannot hear or taste the smoke. I am looking through
the blue light of morning snow as he says he is not good,

he was given a choice. I am in Nebraska City, I am in the basement
and there is smoke. My hand, like a child's, is hovering above the stove.

To Fox Tail, Whose Many Songs Were Taken

In the gift shop, your tail hung disembodied by the register—
priced pom-pom of fur to be bought as a souvenir.

That night I dreamt your body intact, whole again as after-image.
And your nocturne in the den of my liver ever since.

When faced with a downed tree after flooding, you said
the path is my nape. You said to watch the branches

of the Manzanitas, how they balm their fists in pools
of shadow. The scabbing over of lichen in rows.

Everywhere are monuments to survival. Lightning, drought,
wildfire. You said *notice how*, topping a breeze, birds slide,

shuck the pale light off. Trill and tune the air. What moves inside
their bones hovers close to instinct of verse. Of course, you have

no word for it: the flight inside the bird. Keep moss close,
you said, she is lush in her infinite form. Like the sky knows

to stretch and hold the hand of music, the air widens and
the light becomes more than light, deeper than mirror.

Self-Portrait with This Throat and Goodbye

Write this throat into a harp,

this throat, this tin-can

telephone. Turn this loose change

into soft honey. Warm this throat

to make an incubator, to stock a library.

Frame an exhibit with this throat, this collage,

call it *All These Years I Never Said This.*

Call this what it is. The throat,

the road in. Say this throat is

jeweled with fly bites. Over my carotid,

like a right hand over the heart.

Say where it hurts. Show

this throat is rung with bones.

Tell me the why about this:

his name standing up in my throat.

Wring this throat like a rag,

time it ring true. Because this

throat is rusted. Because where

breeze dumb windsock?

Nude this throat, and transparent—

limp leg of a woman's pantyhose.

Say carotid, sung like the name of a star.

String this throat a harp.

Thrash the throat with wonder, this throat

a happy blender. An engine, a rattle,

a locket, a valve, a bridge, a bird.

The burn, the salve, the break, the stint.

Marriage as Migration

It begins, this sprawl.
We unwrap from ourselves
for the uprush,

this ripe haw. Low on
the lawn of the brain
until drafted out

of innocence. The ways
we were: wayfarers,
wave-breakers. But how far

out still keeps true
north? We see where
this is headed, no

unsnarling from this
passage. A haul so run
with distance. Hurled

into exodus, every fall
to fall. Yet there is nest
after rasp of exertion,

lactic acid built up plush.
And so with lunar navigation:
washing in the raw pull

of pulsars. So spurred,
so measured, not arrived
anywhere yet. But

we'll come by way of long
and arduous. This pilgrimage
to pay for allegiance.

After War After War After

You've come home from deployment
but can't rest, you sleep with a radar field

inside your head. You go back there
every night—speak into the old caves,

come out mumbling, talk of elders.
Talk of children begging for candy, calling out

every American piece they knew.
Talk of the boy who was brought to base

with half his small head cleared away
by the blast mine he played with.

You've already been dead. You were gone
so I buried you at my desk and you died

again, again. Your many deaths
showed themselves like cards face up

on the black mantle inside my skull. You
and some explosive device, you

in the radius of its threshing halo. You
legless on the phone, on hold with the VA.

You turning gold then grey, slipped into a black
sleeve and mailed to your last known address.

We are Whispers in a Bedroom Under the Ocean

What I remember most from back then—when we lived
in California, what grows more dense with time—are the hills.

Driving deeper into Camp Pendleton, past
Mainside and Margarita, they would rise up around me
like chins wearing yellow shadows.

How my car ached against the speed limits
before finally I reached inside your jeans

behind the closed door of your barracks room.
How you entered the valley between my hips and spoke
into the sky above the ceiling. How we came loose

inside the bowl the hills made. How the cement walls
seemed to always be leaning in, listening.

And the way the hills sighed into smooth angles along the ocean—
the way it looked in San Clemente when the hills lay down supine
and turned into beaches. Before the deployments.

I remember all the metal, all the shells on those hills.
The stretches of base where your infantry battalion lived

and trained. The hills looking different after you made
your mind up about death. The barracks musky
with the breath of a hundred panting men.

And the night that had no stars, just cement-colored clouds.
The night before you deployed that first time.

I left you at your barracks room, but I didn't drive back home,
past Margarita, past Mainside. I found a tall hill,
dense as a shell pressured into its chamber.

I pulled off the road and parked. I lay down supine

on the hood and wondered about the valleys in the sky,

letting the ache reach me, enter me.
From up there, I spoke into the distance, a dark ceiling.
I could nearly see your barracks room, the smooth angles

of your jeans. If I didn't leave that hill,
that first deployment didn't have to start, didn't have to rise up

around me like closed doors. I imagined opening
the ocean, the blue door to a bedroom.
We were the shadows behind that door—ageless, eating

from the bowl of each other's hands. We whispered,
we panted. I stayed all night on that hill, leaning in, listening.

Ex-Votos for Alcoholism

A long way through sallow hills to Fresno.
Burnt grass reminding me of piss,

then, naturally, jaundice.
Farmland hollowing but is memory

of water. I try not to look
at the carcasses.

But was that owl still dying?
It looked just struck and,

wings flailing, freshly
registering the damage. Or not.

Not an animal showing me
its leaving. A cream wing caught up

by the rush of passing trucks,
life having already evacuated.

Wing in lift because the air,
its hollowness, it must. Can't

remember now where I was
before the owl—the passenger

in my head never looking in
my same direction.

Left are the ledger of miles
after this.

Announcement

My name, from its male origins, meant messenger.

When I said *You ruined me*, I wanted to reverse the word order,
twin the pain and dig it in you.

The angel Gabriel stood two bows-lengths from a prophet,
craved closeness but, by nature, chose instead his secrets.

You once called me *barrier fire*, a barrage. As if looking
in the mirror, I am onslaught. A landslide coming closer.

He was meant to be a comfort to man as he was felled.
Gabriel translated what the earth said, once broken open:

This is in you.

Two by two, we're both no good. We are
the other's flood sentence.

This is done, said Gabriel, *And this is the new.*

II

When I Was Astarte

Holding this bowl beneath my breasts,

the fifteenth of lunar July grows fat

with moony desire. My milk is a miracle. I am sovereign. I wander

and take up with still-born stars. With this head of a bull

as my own, I underpin every galley post, every ibex,

the dusk in the sky, the under-life. The gates to hell

sing to appease me. They meant my name

to mean *shame* but rams grow wombs in my sight,

their fluted horns discarded. And way back,

at the first light, there was an egg on my knee.

From this egg broke twins. They swam past the cloudlets

and seeded this world. One never returned.

And so the living will wilt like petals.

All will scald between my lips, my vessel of annihilation.

But I will regrow those who die in battle, breech

birth, slaughter chutes. This is to become again, climb

back up my branches, taste

the sulfur of matches, reach out and graze

my freckles, field of capsized planets.

Seizures

Strange aches still haunt like riptides,
                pull something dangerous between us.
     Few years have shelled me like these.
        A once singular pain

has rearranged itself into many. You remind me
      that our anatomies
              are just puzzles apt for disassembly.
                   Whose fault is it

that on every bridge I check the height
      of its railing? How under my grip I imagine
          the rain? Is it really me
              when I come home to you, drinking?

When I prefer the suffering of dogs
         to yours? In those moments,
     I am lit with fear, primed
           like a cattle prod and I
       want to flood your head with voltage.

Animals are euthanized every day
     in other countries
          without the aid of intravenous drugs.
              Instead, due to cost, electrocution
        induces a massive coronary.

There's always regret associated
      with learning about our own fallibility.
          And I admit this
between us has changed.
              Though middle summer

trucked in the sun from last year,
     I keep hearing hunted things panting
         in the alley. I keep
             diving past railings in dreams.

The Hypnotist Suggests the Word *History*

Foaled the boys then killed the yearlings. Made men made music. Song the bullets and the bees. Song the spring he saw between them. Song raw opium pods leaked yellow, dried, and looked like burned flesh, burned fat, raw. Opening, so beautiful the Helmand River Valley, he said *almost* he fed the river down from the dam, up the road laced with razor wire, pearled with checkpoints. FOB Zee. Kajaki, poppy, *pretty*, green. *They come to me, we make red lace in the sky*. Sandstorms, gunner, diamond. Taliban found. Their eyes in his before air support unzipped, let down its heavy metal dress. *Taliban dreams drones flown by trained rodents*. Were no words for the word of the river fed fat with mute men, fed flowers, fed opium fields, fed tobacco, fed sugar beets. *Sugar, honey, sweet?* His war never stops never talking, not buying a house not shopping, not home improvements, not termites, not torn steps, eaten siding. From Arabic *sukkar*, from Persian *shaker*. Alexander the Great called it *honey without the bees*.

Bildungsroman

*

I was a child, I was a porcelain bowl
someone washed their hands in

then made to feel responsible
for emptying it. It was handed to me.

It was night, wasted in the sky,
somewhere, still raging,

some dark lake. Because time, because
above is a deep cave.

*

Dead bodies will release
the contents of their bowels in the relaxation

following death. Then like this:
blood pools and settles.

A body's temperature drops
until matching the room it's in.

Skin cells live for days
after this. Cells die individually

so one death is actually many.

*

Children grow deeply anxious
during potty training.

Self-mastery must happen

before a child can be successful.

She is a stranger to her—
she who owns the equipment.

Picturing actions (symbolic thinking)
is new and awareness of her

physical map is an expanse.
The feeling of fullness

is not easily monitored.
By two, she should be able

to control the muscles that expel waste,
delay if not appropriate.

*

Not suicide, not really. I wanted me out of it.
I kept this from myself and everyone so

spoke and erased it, extended my hand behind
entire blank sentences.

*

This dream I have—a public restroom,
row of stalls. Most doors ajar
or ripped from their hinges.

I'm so pressed with need
and frozen in fear of it. Every fluid
a human can void runs down

each bowl. On the floor, dewy
on the ceiling, monstrous, overflowing,
so near me, continuous,

everywhere and no out.
Locked in with myself, mess. Mocked
at the precipice until morning.

*

There were boundaries

and then none, deployments and fracturing
which trained the ease out of me.

I learned nothing. Because it was random,
unseen, violent, forceful, consenting encompassing,

no way to avoid it. Each plane I boarded was ordained
to go down. I was afraid of the silence

after the phone call, the trip to the store,
the odd slip or slur of words which would skid

me into chaos again. What was the name of the pilot?

*

If I was killed skydiving, it would be reported
as an accident. Maybe some small comfort to my family.

I didn't want the choice to be mine. I was tired
of myself and weakness. I liked the giving in to it—

possibility of falling and nothing underneath.
The *What if I die?* which deters most people

making me giddy. And it was like fucking off,
a hard hush. Klonopin freefall,

plugging my ears like I was diving underwater.
The emptying, the open. The rough deaf passing

through me above a lake below a plane vessel
only capable of awe. A note sustained passed wailing.

Bottoming out of an orgasm, blown back. Dumped out.
Time lapse photography of fruit ripening

until it turns back into itself, decays. How a short-fused prayer
sucked out of the lungs is called an ejaculation.

A holy outing, a purge. It was like peeling off
a blue surgical glove. It was like taking a shower.

Options for the Banderole at My Birth

with a century of mantis in her

in the mist of a bandaged moon

for the dead, ancient and hazel

to be sent in a Cessna over Gopher Canyon

dedicated to dogspeak

translated from atmosphere at high altitude

stolen from a once-prominent patch of crabgrass

in which it is always winter

Unmap

Constant state of *what*.

    what wounded.

what of unknown origin.

    what this foreign body.

from a carcass on I-40.

    what lost. *what*

Inhabiting this land

    Living through this *what*,

This hail, my teeth, it grows in me

    this all-inclusive *what*.

goes past me, driving and *what*

    by the throat.

of *what* around the moon.

    hemisphere, I lope.

Lay Down Your *what*

    say Feed Your Strangers,

Fast and metal, this blind

    Little transient

in the deep of the

Word for word for *what*.

Thirst of *what*, tending the fires of *what*.

what a chronic condition.

    what slipping like steam

    what fugitive.

a ran horse emptied.

of *what*.

    snow blindness.

    this snow,

    This whoosh of whoa

    holds me

Chandelier of lightning, lamp

Tide by tide, I tow each blank

On the highway signs say

and be Saved,

    say Hang In There, Baby.

    bomb, I run.

what, I go. Caught

dark, my what

a thousand years   or more—

kingdom of *what*,   place of dazzling

zoologies of *what*,   herds of *what*, flocks of *what*,

stumbling drunk   under the heaven of *what*.

Cathedral hush   and hunting, mapping

and splintering, digging   and burying,

drawn and dawning   on me, a cleft.

what a mirror   and mile marker, portrait gallery

of having left.

We the strays

drop shadows in my dreams.   Lives inside me
roiling—my   gums tinted with them,

my pockets, sleeping in   my acne scars,
      rolling across my twenty knuckles,

my hooded   eyes. Made up of stray
parts, whispered with   them.

What you notice, you will become.
At night they marble   in my jaw.

I   teem, can't   sleep, coughed   up
with them. And if I   vision—

field and appar   itions and
flak and   rain. I tell myself   they need

my help. They ask me   *Who are you*
lost to?   Daily roadside chorus,

chanting: *Just like us, it's someone's*
job to clean you   *r tracks, take*

you u   *p—your shit, your startle,*
your foamy eyes   *not fixed*

on the ho   *me you said could never*
find you. Secrets keep m   e warm,

draw me like   a porch light.
My guilt, my solitary, my   empty

        lot, edges of me frayed,
vigilant. Vacant, moon-   fragrant,

fragmented. I'm   only sure that
we were   born—that single day

our one return.

Leonora Carrington, *The Temptation of St. Anthony*, 1945

Your kiss said rooms of bison, tasting of bright

history—final and rundown. You said nothing

until I roamed to your mouth, your jars, your door

to color. I was not a girl in that room.

You said I was godly, your last. It was the snow

in your empty hands, your fur at midnight—

its black carry. The stars were glands, tic tacs

of light in the sky's worn balcony. I could not contain

my stay for you. You who pinned a ruined prayer

to my collar. Each night was a galloping, a squall-headed

drowning and at morning you'd wake with my salt

on your robes like bread in the mouth of the starving.

Marriage as Hibernation

Our reaping hours
are wintering
behind us now.

Neurons now
a thicket of blank
gestures. Torpor now.

Cold now dropping
its deep auger.
We low

our heads down.
We conserve
memories of

once-clotted rivers
to dampen
our dreams. Reams

of wrecked light
where once we were
sharpened.

Outside,
wasps are loaded
in their nests.

This dormancy
is open-ended.
This slog

has worn us out.
Time torn. And so
surrender.

Our tongues
dissolve like time-
release capsules.

And so nod
to the nervous
code of rain.

Veterans Day at the Fresno Community Hospital

After fire, comes flood.   After blast, comes more
bomb—more scrap that didn't catch bone the first time.

What had begun grinding towards you since your birth,
met you   with the force of eventuality.

Like memories you'd tried to core out on purpose,
like a biopsy.   They called me because you had converged

with it all at once. They called it   *psychosis.*
I drove untethered for those days, waiting for it

to burn out like a fever. Medically, it wasn't
nearly so simple.   I swallowed Xanax dryly, unsure

if I should drive. Drained my tank drifting in and out
of exits in a town foreign to me.   That dead shepherd

decomposing on the freeway.   Bound by leather restraints
in the ambulance, you whispered that I poisoned the water.

And at the hospital I would be turned away.   It took two days
for the doctors to release your information because

you told them I was dead.   I drove to Woodward Park
and nearly fell each step I took.   Branches cluttered

the sun.　　　　Children crawled into the lake.　　　Hunger's noose
around my waist.　　　　Day-ache siren.　　　Pulse-tangled knots

in my wrists.　　　Minutes held the gravity of planets.
Tell me again how you thought they were putting you down.

Euthanasia for a horse　　　　with a twisted stomach.
You came home covered in bruises　　　　and loosely connected.

Convinced　　　your roommate was Satan,
you wondered aloud if hospitalization was　　　a test.

You said Satan　　　sent you telekinetic threats, said he knew
Veterans Day had something to do with it.　　　I know

my joints are close　　　but they feel far.　　　Like hunger,
it's a reaction to emptiness.　　　Lack-making. Unstructured time.

If I were to graph that day on a timeline,　　　Y-axis measuring
depth of feeling and X-axis time　　　towards infinity—

a plot above the line would represent　　　a kindness,
a blot below, a blow.　　　The dots wouldn't connect,

wouldn't create a constellation.　　　They'd just be bullets
that didn't connect, didn't leave holes　　　in anybody.

The Animal Afterward

When all the milk teeth have fallen
    and our gums are fresh, wet,
raw—when the calcification has begun
    to fuse one rib and a digit
to the next—when the sun bleaches
    our skull matte—when sand
has rubbed the rest of us smooth,
    we can shed our outer
wounds, the matted tufts too tough
    to pass off as skin.
And then burrow in each other,
    the only other—
the I, the you. How long ago
    was the first season,
our first spring—my first nest
    hairy with bees?
We stalked each other, our only
    other, held down
with stiff spine, stuck need.
    It was the prologue with limbs.
And I've kept every tooth,
    veins dried inside them.
Pinned up the slough to the walls
    inside me in rows
like roses. I've slept with clippings
    of your whiskers braided
into the hem of my sheets. You've
    left traces of your claws,
marked me in stripes you'd find
    only on a fish. We will
always have each other like this.
    Leviathan and Behemoth—
us in the beginning, us meeting
    the end and starting again.
After our epoch they'll find us
    as skeletons under the ocean,

water will peel away to show
   what we had been.
We'll be raw bones, but again,
   we'll have breath.

Archetype

Horses on the ridge
                 when I'm finally sleeping,

long diamonds on their faces.

         They smell like dung and star anise.

They bow to the palace
                 of shadows that a dream is.

Up and over the ridge is Satan,

            a lonely horse himself.

I can only tell his face
                 is lovely, tender knobs

rise from his forehead.

He lets me listen to his thoughts with him,

         how he turns each phrase

like a mirror up to his face.   *Once I was an angel,*

then I was a snake.
            I came to Eve because she was

         as I was—drawn to solitude,

warmth, the light

blinking inside her own mind.

                 He stands

on his hind legs to assess
                    the crop of dreamers

watching him. I look to him

        like a floating staircase, smoke framing

a mouth. I wander towards
                    waking awhile

before looking back at the ridge, the fallen.

        Satan calls out to ask me
                    if I thought choice

was just a fallacy.   As if

Eve thought twice

            to follow the horses wherever

                        they were going.

M-16

"My rifle is human, even as I, because it is my life.
I will keep my rifle clean and ready, even as I am clean
and ready. We will become part of each other."
– The Rifleman's Creed

I've heard the trigger is a metaphor

for a woman's clitoris, a snake's tongue

locked in hiss. My husband's gun is human,

because he is. Not fitted with his fists,

she is simply a slender neck,

her mouth

the opening of a star.

When she flashes teeth,

they swallow sky. It's called thieving.

I forgive her: she is the matte black animal

without the consciousness of eyes.

The Poet Says Her Vows

Look at me: A wordy thread, a red mess
    sewn around a diamond.

Preoccupied as pulp with rind,
    I will flay this skin right

open. Only with my teeth.
    Lucky like a bright house key

because I am woman made
    from woman. Inherited folk tongue,

was caught teaching crow.
    Sacred cow of grasses,

doll with fork and spoon.
    I am innumerable

rubs of worry, rubs of worry
    count by twos. Two for me,

me for you. Our thin-stem flowers
    have bloomed, pistils ripened,

each petal new. On the flowers shine,
    at night iced by the prick of stars.

My breasts a vegetable garden,
    a path for the fat and new

to take root. My spine
    a fence post, a weird litany.

And my need like whale, like
    fox is need. I am

dream and anxious insect. I pace
    our home's pelvic floor.

And I am constant genitals thinking
    of themselves, glowing like an atom

bomb, full-on in range of you.
    I am that blinky satellite tranced

in orbit around you. You
    is a world unto itself, the other

island in the ocean. Between us, blue.
    Come here *potato*.

Get on top, *dark ceiling*.
    Dear *lonely*, take me with you.

I am a forest thick with drought
    for you. I am woman and blood

is my inheritance. So it is. So it must.
    Hear, the wolves are calling,

searching out their mating pair.
    For years and years, my *consecrate*.

My *heart*, honeycombed with darkness.
    Meet me after slaughter's done,

after summer killing
    ended and blessed you.

I am a babbler of some other world,
    and I am yours there, too.

The Hypnotist Suggests the Word *Home*

Labyrinth, rapture, salvo. The release, all at once, a rack of rockets, a salve. Dismantling the elk nest, ants in the scaffolding of our bed. Of ruin. Of run. Of our mouths—like mountains—damp and dancing with silence. The first story I told: *The VA gave him a 100% disability rating.* Addresses given, gone defunct, turned black, amputated. Addresses long hemmed in our guts like heat, hardening at our center like diamonds. *Deployment after deployment, diagnosis. Called condition.* The outline in the doorway after dreaming. The distances crossed. We called it *going* to forget *gone*. A training. Opposite of occupation. We called it *occupation* to forget *waiting.* The small herd pact, the smell of us settling on the grass. *What could we have done?* As in, removed from. As in, caged up / set free. As in, *we. He said his stories have become our stories.* From Italian *salva*, from French *salve*, from Latin, *hail!*, from *salvus*, meaning *health.* The first story is always about naming, creating—the genesis of voice.

To Ghost Tongue with the Body of a Fawn

Made of milk, made of ash, flame-colored fur, you speak
like Cholla flowers. Your voice a portrait of presence

and empty—a desert. A palette. Unending stretches gone velvet with rain.
Come home to me, I can't reach you. Begin in me a blue agave, harvest

the heart by morning. Smear sap on my mouth. Say something.
I've heard you call up tall mountains, thicken forests, adorn each silent one

with a name. When I would sleep, you'd fit arenas in the sky, star stadiums
like an echo. Assign each water moon a pool. You'd come to me,

I'd taste syllables in your fur, pick pinned pearls from your back.
You'd say sound was born from the word *persimmon*. I could never doubt you.

But you haven't been near, where are you? How I beg
to be the canoe that carries you, ocean a curtain of hair. To speak of you,

be your mandible—egg-shell shovel—eat again those pallets of fire.
This morning I am hungry. I have not eaten.

Unopened blossoms in the warehouse of my tongue.
Bright bell, swing before the flowers. Tell.

Poem Where My Nose Gets Broken

You were afraid they'd think you hit me,
bag of frozen corn on my nose in the ER.

They read the rough of your knuckles
when I said it was your elbow, an accident—

I was right behind you as you were lifting
my old writing desk. Your hair marked you

a jarhead and the hospital, the officer saw
the blood, your body next to mine

in the waiting room. The way they watched you.
Their eyes unblinking, glowing like projector screens.

The year before, a man at a bar explained to me
all Marines join to satisfy a lust to kill for money.

A bank teller asked me if you enlisted
because you couldn't get into college.

I shouldn't have been surprised by it—
how drunk and shrunken under grief

you got after the hospital. Yet, I too, am just a civilian.
I've heard it said that humans can't truly know

each other—all we have is language. All I know
is what you tell me. That night you said war

is like flying without an airplane, your hands
around an invisible wheel of air. Control is a need

of the mind, intangible and nourishing, vanishing,
and not real. I've heard it said in art,

a direct gaze is considered confrontational,
can be seen as erotic. I look into the glossy stare

of your boot camp portrait that sits
on my new writing desk, watches as I write this.

I wonder about you, just nineteen then.
Nothing for you to know beyond

the pose before the lens, the camera's flash
fashioning you into a fixed image. The stories

you told yourself were rounds still neat
in their casings. And then what came next.

Epilogue for the Fall

Face the fire left in these embers—your presence
will act as kindling. Look at your reflection

in the blue pit of flame, the green in it an Eden.
Don't listen to the paranoid yips of the jackals

all around us, their calls eating through
the lacquered quiet of this night. Never mind fever,

never mind this raw winter. Never mind I said
evil was like a kiss—shared between two people.

I saw your hands not used to stillness and thought
I had to fill them with definitions, my own

disturbances. I heard your voice directionless
as you said a man cannot unmake his hands

for war and his fingers for battle. You tried
distraction. Tried swallowing sunlight off the glint

of a barrel. Said inside you was an absence.
The film of a violent year. Blood and its echo.

I want you to know that blood is us, our anthem.
The steady hum in the din of wilderness,

that chorus which clamps us hard between horizon
and the riotous sky. Same as what fastens the tremble

to my voice. For we are now as we were always—warped
into the rings of a tree, the crook in a track of lightning.

The ranger in a pack of wolves. The lamb harvested
whole from its belly. Even these ashes.

Psalm of the Firestarter

Winds don't enter the church
I built and condemned inside myself.

I was taught a woman's body
was reared to bear secrets—

some that should stay a mystery,
even to her. Like when

an animal looks in the mirror
and doesn't recognize a self.

As children we learn to beg,
say *yes*. We file out of the chapels

and the classrooms
and learn to spill into lovers,

bur their lips with our phobias,
our leper dreams.

To close off our hearts,
that deep closet of flame.

We start to crave the lash
of nightmares. Imagine

licking up walls, buckling them—
hot with the crush of ignition.

I fled to oceans, I wandered
and found flesh—

some to eat, some to undress.
I fed all of my disappearances.

I destroyed a holy city
someone said was inside me.

Because the Lord used
my heat to accompany music,

because the Lord adorned
my hair with horns.

Because to be penitent
meant being penitent.

How Woman Inherits the Earth

Come some blood, some gristle. Let myself be unfurled,
red tongue rolled out, wine-thick, a wave.

Speak myself into existence. Open wide the cage inside me,
survey my boning, my nerve, the lit lace of me.

Not long before the thaw, I was carved, crushed as snow.
Was made to shatter, was ice. Underground spring turned hungry,

I turned mindless fog, spirit in the grass. I rinsed myself thin like droplets.
I could hear myself disappearing—erasure—back into a cloud.

Back to phantom lung, gauze unpacked from snow, silver beaded shadow,
white liver, frost tongue. Now long pastures of my voice unveil themselves

by lightning. The net of veins, damp ribbons in my chest, untie
their knots—I sing. I breathe— my lungs patterned after

two warped mandolins. My limbs—unfolded maps of open water.
Come some sound, some answer. Come the cells that build the blood,

the crumbs of notes in music. Let not my fear, my love for this world
be a coagulant. Let me bring it to my lips and drink.

Acknowledgements

Big, big thanks to the editors of the following journals in which my poems have appeared, sometimes in different forms:

The Adroit Journal: "Ex-Votos for Alcoholism," "When I Was Astarte," and "Archetype"
Bat City Review: "Bildungsroman"
The Boiler: "Leonora Carrington, *The Temptation of St. Anthony*, 1945"
The Cincinnati Review: "Marriage as Hibernation"
The Collagist: "What Apocalypse"
Columbia Journal: "The Hypnotist Suggests the Word *Home*" and "Unmap"
Crazyhorse: "Marriage An Animal Language"
Devil's Lake: "The Body's Law Transcribed from Darkness"
DIALOGIST: "Parasomnia"
Fifth Wednesday Journal: "We are Whispers in a Bedroom Under the Ocean"
Frontier Poetry: "Frida Kahlo, *The Little Deer*, 1946"
The Georgia Review: "Écorché with Terminal Ballistics"
Guernica: "Psalm of the Firestarter"
Indiana Review: "After War After War After" and "Marriage a Pair of Wild Dogs" and "To Ghost Tongue with the Body of a Fawn"
The Journal: "The Poet Says Her Vows"
Mid-American Review: "Epilogue for the Fall" and "Nebraska City"
The Normal School: "Poem Where My Nose Gets Broken" and "Fracturing Travelogue"
Passages North: "The Animal Afterword"
Phoebe: "How Woman Inherits the Earth" and "Helmand Province"
Plume Poetry Journal: "Poem Beginning with a Line from Levis"
Poetry Northwest: "Announcement"
Raleigh Review: "To Fox Tail, Whose Many Songs Were Taken"
Salamander: "M-16"
Sou'wester: "Self-Portrait with This Throat and Goodbye"
Sycamore Review: "The Hypnotist Suggests the Word *History*" and "The Hypnotist Suggests the Word *Hunger*"
Third Point Press: "Marriage as Migration"

"Marriage An Animal Language" was reprinted in *Best New Poets* (2014); "Marriage a Pair of Wild Dogs," "The Animal Afterward," and "How Woman Inherits the Earth" were reprinted in *The Adroit Journal* (2020).

Thank you

This book has been in my head and my laptop for almost ten years and I'm so grateful to hold it in my hands now. Many have helped and supported and validated and encouraged and loved me all along the way. This is for you.

Thank you to The Travelers' Club: Regina DiPerna, Nathan Johnson, Whitney Lawson, Anna B. Sutton, and Eric Tran. You've saved me. I love you.

Thank you to the editors, staff, and volunteers at Trio House Press and Sandy Longhorn for believing in this book. Your support of my work and what you do for the poetry community has been everything.

Thank you to my mentors and teachers who gave me the gift of taking me and my work seriously, even at the earliest stages of my development as a writer. Thank you especially to Sarah Messer. Thank you to Lavonne Adams, Malena Mörling, Rebecca Lee, Wendy Brenner, Nina de Gramont, and the rest of the faculty and staff at the University of North Carolina Wilmington who were good to me during my time in the MFA program. Thank you as well to the brilliant, wild, talented, and generous folks in workshop whose feedback helped me and my poems grow stronger.

Thank you to the following institutions for providing time, space, and funding to work on these poems: The Community of Writers Workshop, the Hedgebrook Writer in Residence program, the Kimmel Harding Nelson Center for the Arts, and Sewanee Writers' Conference.

Thank you to the following poets and platforms for your generous attention and time: Peter LaBerg and *The Adroit Journal*, Jazzy Danziger and *Best New Poets*, Dorianne Laux, Claudia Emerson, Emily Rosko and *Crazyhorse*, Sharon Olds, Mary Ruefle, Christina Stoddard, and the San Diego State University English and Creative Writing Departments.

And thank you to Cyborg, Lil Sebastian, and Frida. My wild pack of family dogs.

About the Author

Gabriella R. Tallmadge is a Latinx writer and educator from San Diego, California. She holds degrees in English, Creative Writing, and Counseling. She is also certified in Mental Health Recovery and Trauma-Informed Care by San Diego State University. Gabriella's poetry has received awards from the Hedgebrook Writer in Residence Program, the Community of Writers Workshop, the Kimmel Harding Nelson Center for the Arts, and Sewanee Writers' Conference. Her work has previously appeared in journals such as *The Adroit Journal*, *The Georgia Review*, *Crazyhorse*, *Guernica*, *Mid-American Review*, and *Passages North*. To learn more, visit www. grtallmadge.com.

About the Artist

"My name is Aniko and I'm an artist from a magical place surrounded by lakes and mysterious forests. I aim to transfer the emotion of unconditional love, absolute bliss, and divine power through my art. Guiding with my work to awaken the authentic self. Also, believing in magic that is unseen with a bare eye, but strongly felt within. I come to think that the work I create has a message of its own that wants to spread and reach people the intuitive feeling of interconnectedness between the Universe, Nature, every single thing orbiting around your life path and YOU. Being a part of it all, feeling comfortable with waving your existence away in the vast cosmos of the Unknown. www.anikoarts.com"

About the Book

Sweet Beast was designed at Trio House Press through the collaboration of:

Matt Mauch, Lead Editor
Sara Lefsyk, Supporting Editor
Aniko, Joel Coggins, Cover Design
Matt Mauch, Interior Design

The text is set in Adobe Caslon Pro.

The publication of this book is made possible, whole or in part,
by the generous support of the following individuals or agencies:

Anonymous

About the Press

Trio House Press is an independent literary press publishing three or more collections of poems annually. Our Mission is to promote poetry as a literary art enhancing culture and the human experience. We offer two annual poetry awards: the Trio Award for First or Second Book for emerging poets and the Louise Bogan Award for Artistic Merit and Excellence for a book of poems contributing in an innovative and distinct way to poetry. We also offer an annual open reading period for manuscript publication.

Trio House Press adheres to and supports all ethical standards and guidelines outlined by the CLMP.

Trio House Press, Inc. is dedicated to the promotion of poetry as literary art, which enhances the human experience and its culture. We contribute in an innovative and distinct way to poetry by publishing emerging and established poets, providing educational materials, and fostering the artistic process of writing poetry. For further information, or to consider making a donation to Trio House Press, please visit us online at www.triohousepress.org.

Other Trio House Press books you might enjoy:

The Traditional Feel of the Ballroom by Hannah Rebecca Gamble / 2021

Third Winter in Our Second Country by Andres Rojas / 2021

Songbox by Kirk Wilson / 2020 Trio Award Winner selected by Malena Mörling

YOU DO NOT HAVE TO BE GOOD by Madeleine Barnes / 2020

X-Rays and Other Landscapes by Kyle McCord / 2019

Threed, This Road Not Damascus by Tamara J. Madison / 2019

My Afmerica by Artress Bethany White / 2018 Trio Award Winner selected by Sun Yung Shin

Waiting for the Wreck to Burn by Michele Battiste / 2018 Louise Bogan Award Winner selected by Jeff Friedman

Cleave by Pamel Johnson Parker / 2018 Trio Award Winner selected by Jennifer Barber

Two Towns Over by Darren C. Demaree / 2018 Louise Bogan Award Winner selected by Campbell McGrath

Bird~Brain by Matt Mauch / 2017

Dark Tussock Moth by Mary Cisper / 2016 Trio Award Winner selcted by Bhisham Bherwani

The Short Drive Home by Joe Osterhaus / 2016 Louise Bogan Award Winner selected by Chard DeNiord

Break the Habit by Tara Betts / 2016

Bone Music by Stephen Cramer / 2015 Louise Bogan Award Winner selected by Kimiko Hahn

Rigging a Chevy into a Time Machine and Other Ways to Escape a Plague by Carolyn Hembree / 2015 Trio Award Winner selected by Neil Shepard

Magpies in the Valley of Oleanders by Kyle McCord / 2015

Your Immaculate Heart by Annmarie O'Connell / 2015

The Alchemy of My Mortal Form by Sandy Longhorn / 2014 Louise Bogan Award Winner selected by Peter Campion

What the Night Numbered by Bradford Tice / 2014 Trio Award Winner selected by Carol Frost

Flight of August by Lawrence Eby / 2013 Louise Bogan Award Winner selected by Joan Houlihan

The Consolations by John W. Evans / 2013 Trio Award Winner selected by Mihaela Moscaliuc

Fellow Odd Fellow by Stephen Riel / 2013

Clay by David Groff / 2012 Louise Bogan Award Winner selected by Michael Waters

Gold Passage by Iris Jamahl Dunkle / 2012 Trio Award Winner selected by Ross Gay

If You're Lucky Is a Theory of Mine by Matt Mauch / 2012

CPSIA information can be obtained
at www.ICGtesting.com
Printed in the USA
JSHW021823160521
14732JS00006B/8